I0096360

TSW Publishing
P. O. Box 176
Centreville, Virginia 20122
www.scholarshipworkshop.com
TSW Publishing is a division of The Scholarship Workshop LLC

Copyright © 2024 by Marianne Ragins
All rights reserved. No part of this publication may be used or reproduced in any manner whatsoever without prior written consent of the author, except as provided by the United States of America copyright law.

The Scholarship Monthly Planner was written to provide accurate advice to readers. However, please note that the author nor the publisher are engaged in the practice of providing legal, accounting, tax or other professional advice. If you need legal, accounting, tax or other advice, please consult a professional in the appropriate area. Neither the author, the publisher, nor any entity associated with *The Scholarship Monthly Planner* assume any liability for errors, omissions, or inaccuracies. Any action you take or do not take as a result of reading *The Scholarship Monthly Planner* is entirely your responsibility.

ISBN: 978-1-950653-21-8

Printed in the United States of America

This resource is available at special quantity discounts for bulk purchases for sales promotions, premiums, fundraising, and educational use. Special versions or excerpts can also be created to fit specific needs.

For more information, please contact info@scholarshipworkshop.com or call 703 579-4245. You can also write: TSW Publishing, P. O. Box 176, Centreville, Virginia 20122.

The Scholarship Monthly Planner
2024-2025

The Scholarship Monthly Planner

August 2024

SUN	MON	TUE	WED	THU	FRI	SAT
When visiting websites, you may need to use the search box on the site or through the home page to find the specific scholarship program listed.	.Work on your scholarship résumé/ extracurricular activity, honors, and awards list.	Look at all deadlines for upcoming scholarships you've already researched. Be sure they are included in your calendar.	*Check website for VFW Patriot's Pen Essay Contest rules — https://www.vfw.org/community/youth-and-education/youth-scholarships ——— Check website for application: Coca-Cola Scholars Foundation — www.coca-colascholarsfoundation.org	**1** Tylenol Future Care Scholarship Program application due soon — www.tylenol.com/news/subptyschol) ——— *Begin working on Ayn Rand "Atlas Shrugged" Essay Contest entry — https://aynrand.org/students/essay-contests	**2** Check website for Gates Scholarship Application — https://www.thegatesscholarship.org/scholarship ——— **Check website for Americanism Educational Leaders Essay Contest — https://infoguides.pepperdine.edu/AEL	**3** Check website for Regeneron Science Talent Search process and rules — https://student.societyforscience.org/regeneron-sts ——— Check website for United States Senate Youth Program application process and regional deadlines — http://ussenateyouth.org
4 Check website for National YoungArts Foundation competition entry rules — www.youngarts.org ——— **Check website for Scholarship America Dream Award Application — https://scholarshipamerica.org/students/browse-scholarships/apply-for-the-dream-award	**5** Contact your local American Legion chapter for information on The American Legion National High School Oratorical Contest — www.legion.org	**6** **Check website for TE Connectivity African Heritage Scholarship Program application — https://learnmore.scholarsapply.org/teconnectivity-african-heritage	**7** Check website for entry rules: American Fire Sprinkler Association Second Chance Scholarship Contest — www.afsascholarship.org (FOR NONTRADITIONAL STUDENTS) Also see @afsascholarship or www.facebook.com/afsascholarship/	**8** Check website for Prudential Emerging Visionaries process (formerly Prudential Spirit of Community Award) — https://www.prudential.com/links/about/emergingvisionaries (OPEN TO STUDENTS AGES 14 TO 18)	**9** Check website for Davidson Fellows Scholarship application process — http://www.davidsongifted.org/Fellows-Scholarship (OPEN TO ALL STUDENTS UNDER AGE 18)	**10**
11 Check website for QuestBridge National College Match application process — www.questbridge.org Also see www.facebook.com/questbridge	**12** +Check website for The Christophers Annual Video Contest — https://www.christophers.org/video-contest-for-college-students or https://www.christophers.org	**13** Check website for the Anne Ford Scholarship application — www.ncld.org	**14** ***Check website for Beinecke Scholarship nomination process — https://beineckescholarship.org	**15** **DO THIS NOW!** Review scholarship résumé/activity list for areas to improve such as community service, leadership, overall involvement. A well-rounded student has a better chance of winning scholarships.	**16** Check website for entry kit: Toshiba NSTA ExploraVision Awards — www.exploravision.org (OPEN TO STUDENTS IN GRADES K—12)	**17** Check website for Soroptimist Live Your Dream Awards — https://www.soroptimist.org/our-work/live-your-dream-awards (OPEN TO WOMEN WHO ARE PRIMARY FINIANCIAL SUPPORT FOR THEIR HOUSEHOLD)
18 *Check website Don't Text and Drive Scholarship entry rules — www.digitalresponsibility.org/dont-text-and-drive-scholarship	**19** *+Check website for application: Ronald V. Dellums Memorial SMART Scholarship Program — https://www.smartscholarship.org/smart	**20** Check with your student chapter advisor: DECA Scholarship Program — www.deca.org/scholarships	**21** +Check website for application: SMART Scholarship Program — https://www.smartscholarship.org/smart	**22** Check website for Gates Scholarship Application — https://www.thegatesscholarship.org	**23** Check website for entry rules: American Fire Sprinkler Association High School Seniors Scholarship Contest — www.afsascholarship.org (FOR NONTRADITIONAL STUDENTS) Also see @afsascholarship or www.facebook.com/afsascholarship	**24** If you are a junior, start preparing for the PSAT which may be given by your high school in October.
25 Contact the National Society of the Daughters of the American Revolution (NSDAR) for information about their scholarship programs — www.dar.org or https://dar.academicworks.com	**26** Contact your local American Legion chapter for information on The American Legion National High School Oratorical Contest — www.legion.org	**27** Check website for Hispanic Heritage Youth Awards application — https://hispanicheritage.org/programs/leadership/youth-awards	**28** Check website for Chick-fil-A Community Scholarship — https://www.chick-fil-a.com/communityscholars	**29** Check website: Brave of Heart Scholarship Program application — https://learnmore.scholarsapply.org/braveofheart/	**30**	**31** Americanism Educational Leaders Essay Contest entry due — https://infoguides.pepperdine.edu/AEL

*Programs are open to current college students and high school seniors.

**Programs are open to current college students only.

***Programs are open to graduate and/or professional school students only.

+Program open to graduate and undergraduate students

Unless otherwise noted, all other programs are open to high school seniors.

Copyright © 2024
The Scholarship Workshop LLC • P. O. Box 176 • Centreville, Virginia 20122 • www.scholarshipworkshop.com

The Scholarship Monthly Planner

Notes

DON'T FORGET!

- Final deadline dates have red text.
- Submit your application at least 7 days before the deadline.
- Always look at least 1 month ahead to get prepared for upcoming deadlines.
- Hate writing? Start on your essay at least 1 month prior to the deadline.
- Need recommendations? Ask at least 4 weeks prior to the deadline. Follow-up! Also, many programs request recommendations electronically. Please let someone know you've provided their e-mail address for a recommendation, so they will be prepared for the e-mail request.
- As you download applications, organize them. You should have one folder for each month. Place applications in the appropriate folder for each month. For example, all applications that are due in December should be in a folder marked December.
- Check previous months for application download dates or activities you need to complete. These activities are shown in black text. Although you may be behind with some activities, the deadline date for a scholarship or award may not have passed.
- Research and include local, regional, and state based scholarships in your calendar.
- Research and include scholarships based on your interests, personal characteristics, and situation in your calendar.
- Request nominations with a letter and your résumé.

Copyright © 2024
The Scholarship Workshop LLC • P. O. Box 176 • Centreville, Virginia 20122 • www.scholarshipworkshop.com

The Scholarship Monthly Planner
September 2024

Left margin notes:

*Programs are open to current college students and high school seniors.

**Programs are open to current college students only.

***Programs are open to graduate and/or professional school students only.

+Program open to graduate and undergraduate students

Unless otherwise noted, all other programs are open to high school seniors.

SUN	MON	TUE	WED	THU	FRI	SAT
When visiting websites, you may need to use the search box on the site or scroll through the home page to find the specific scholarship program listed. *To get alerts of upcoming deadlines and new scholarship opportunities, like The Scholarship Workshop on Facebook or follow us @ScholarshipWork on Twitter and @ScholarshipWorkshop on Instagram.* *You can also visit www.scholarshipworkshop.com/newsletter to join our mailing list for updates!*				Scan this QR code to visit our website for additional information and resources.	Check website for National Beta Club scholarship application — www.betaclub.org/scholarship ———— Check website for application: Elks Most Valuable Student Contest — www.elks.org/enf/scholars/mvs.cfm or contact your local Elks lodge	Check website for application: Equitable Excellence Scholarship— https://equitable.com/foundation/equitable-excellence-scholarship ———— Check website for Ron Brown Scholarship application — www.ronbrown.org
1 American Fire Sprinkler Association Second Chance Scholarship Contest entry due — www.afsascholarship.org (FOR NONTRADITIONAL STUDENTS) Also see @afsascholarship or www.facebook.com/afsascholarship	**2** ***Check website for GEM fellowship application— www.gemfellowship.org ———— Check website for rules: American Fire Sprinkler Association High School Senior Scholarship Contest — www.afsascholarship.org	**3** **Check website for Jack Kent Cooke Undergraduate Transfer Scholarship application — www.jkcf.org Check website for application process and regional deadline: Junior Science and Humanities Symposium (JSHS) Program — www.jshs.org (OPEN TO GRADES 9 THRU 12)	**4** **Check website for Scholarship America Dream Award Application — https://scholarshipamerica.org/students/browse-scholarships/apply-for-the-dream-award	**5** Check website for Jack Kent Cooke College Scholarship Program application — www.jkcf.org *Begin working on Ayn Rand "Atlas Shrugged" Essay Contest entry — https://aynrand.org/students/essay-contests	**6** **Contact dean's office or department chair for nomination process: Coca-Cola Community College Academic Team Scholarship — www.ptk.org (See Scholarships)	**7** Check website for application: Scholastic Art and Writing Awards — www.artandwriting.org (OPEN TO GRADES 7 THRU 12)
8 Contact your local American Legion chapter for information on The American Legion National High School Oratorical Contest — www.legion.org	**9** Check website for The Christophers Annual Poster Contest — https://www.christophers.org/poster-contest or https://www.christophers.org (OPEN TO STUDENTS IN GRADES 9 THRU 12)	**10** **Check website for Coupons Plus Deals Scholarship—https://www.couponsplusdeals.com/scholarship (OPEN TO 3RD OR 4TH YEAR COLLEGE STUDENTS)	**11** Check website for Mu Alpha Theta Kalin Award nomination process — https://mualphatheta.org/kalin_award	**12** Check website: Dr. Arnita Young Boswell Scholarship — www.nhbwinc.com or https://nhbwinc.org/scholarships	**13** Ayn Rand "The Fountainhead" Essay Contest entries due — www.aynrand.org (OPEN TO MIDDLE AND HIGH SCHOOL STUDENTS AGE 13 AND OLDER)	**14** Check website for C-Span's StudentCam competition — http://www.studentcam.org (OPEN TO STUDENTS IN GRADES 6 THRU 12)
15 Gates Scholarship Application due — https://www.thegatesscholarship.org	**16** Check website for application: Coca-Cola Scholars Foundation — www.coca-colascholarsfoundation.org	**17** Check website for entry kit: Toshiba NSTA ExploraVision Awards — www.exploravision.org (OPEN TO STUDENTS IN GRADES K—12)	**18** Check website for National Security Agency Stokes Educational Scholarship Program application — https://www.intelligencecareers.gov/NSA/students-and-internships	**19** Check out College Board Opportunity Scholarships — https://opportunity.collegeboard.org/home	**20** Ayn Rand "Atlas Shrugged" Essay Contest entry due — https://aynrand.org/students/essay-contests/	**21** Check website for John F. Kennedy Profile in Courage Essay Contest rules — www.jfklibrary.org (OPEN TO GRADES 9 THRU 12
22 Check website for Unigo $10,000 Scholarship — https://www.unigo.com/scholarships/our-scholarships/unigo-10k-scholarship (OPEN TO STUDENTS AGE 14 AND UP)	**23** *Check website for Create-A-Greeting-Card Scholarship Contest entry rules — www.gallerycollection.com/greetingcardscontests.htm (OPEN TO NONTRADITIONAL STUDENTS)	**24** Consider applying early for the Equitable Excellence Scholarship (there may be an application limit)— https://equitable.com/foundation/equitable-excellence-scholarship	**25** Check website for Regeneron Science Talent Search process and rules — https://student.societyforscience.org/regeneron-sts	**26** QuestBridge National College Match application due — www.questbridge.org Also see www.facebook.com/questbridge	**27** Check with your student chapter advisor: DECA Scholarship Program — www.deca.org/scholarships	**28** Get a head start on college and scholarship essays with The Scholarship and College Essay Writing Boot Camp! See www.scholarshipworkshop.com or scan this QR Code.
29 *Don't Text and Drive Scholarship deadline SEPTEMBER 30 — www.digitalresponsibility.org/dont-text-and-drive-scholarship/	**30** Coca-Cola Scholarship application due — www.coca-colascholarsfoundation.org/					

Copyright © 2024
The Scholarship Workshop LLC • P. O. Box 176 • Centreville, Virginia 20122 • www.scholarshipworkshop.com

The Scholarship Monthly Planner

Notes

DON'T FORGET!

- Final deadline dates have red text.
- Submit your application at least 7 days before the deadline.
- Always look at least 1 month ahead to get prepared for upcoming deadlines.
- Hate writing? Start on your essay at least 1 month prior to the deadline.
- Need recommendations? Ask at least 4 weeks prior to the deadline. Follow-up! Also, many programs request recommendations electronically. Please let someone know you've provided their e-mail address for a recommendation, so they will be prepared for the e-mail request.
- As you download applications, organize them. You should have one folder for each month. Place applications in the appropriate folder for each month. For example, all applications that are due in December should be in a folder marked December.
- Check previous months for application download dates or activities you need to complete. These activities are shown in black text. Although you may be behind with some activities, the deadline date for a scholarship or award may not have passed.
- Research and include local, regional, and state based scholarships in your calendar.
- Research and include scholarships based on your interests, personal characteristics, and situation in your calendar.
- Request nominations with a letter and your résumé.

The Scholarship Monthly Planner

October 2024

*Programs are open to current college students and high school seniors.

**Programs are open to current college students only.

***Programs are open to graduate and/or professional school students only.

+Program open to graduate and undergraduate students

Unless otherwise noted, all other programs are open to high school seniors.

SUN	MON	TUE	WED	THU	FRI	SAT
If you are a high school junior, get ready to take the PSAT this month. Scoring well among students in your state could qualify you for a National Merit scholarship.	Contact your local Optimist Club for information about the Optimist International Essay and Oratorical Contests — www.optimist.org or https://www.optimist.org/member/scholarships1.cfm (OPEN TO STUDENTS UNDER AGE 19)	**1** ***Check website for GEM fellowship application— www.gemfellowship.org	**2** **Check website for TE Connectivity African Heritage Scholarship Program application — https://learn-more.scholarsapply.org/teconnectivity-african-heritage/	**3** Contact the National Society of the Daughters of the American Revolution (NSDAR) for information about their scholarship programs — www.dar.org or https://dar.academicworks.com	**4** Brave of Heart Scholarship Program application due — https://learn-more.scholarsapply.org/braveofheart/	**5** ***Contact your medical school's dean, student affairs or financial aid office to be considered for an AMA Foundation scholarship nomination — https://amafoundation.org/programs/scholarships
6 Hispanic Heritage Youth Awards application due soon — https://hispanicheritage.org/programs/leadership/youth-awards/	**7** Check website: Stop Hunger Scholarship Program application and deadline — www.sodexofoundation.org or http://us.stop-hunger.org/home/grants.html	**8** Check website for The Google Lime Scholarship — https://edu.google.com/scholarships/the-google-lime-scholarship/ (OPEN TO STUDENTS WITH DISABILITIES)	**9** +Check website for American Association on Health & Disability Scholarship Program— https://www.aahd.us/initiatives/scholarship-program/ (OPEN TO STUDENTS WITH DISABILITIES)	**10** Check website for Dell Scholarship Program application — www.dellscholars.org	**11** Get sponsor for — www.fra.org (see Events and Programs < Americanism Essay Contest) (OPEN TO GRADES 7 THRU 12) Deadline for sponsored entries December 1.	**12** Start working on your Free application for Federal Student Aid (FAFSA) — https://studentaid.gov/h/apply-for-aid/fafsa Also contact schools and states for their specific
13 Check out College Board Opportunity Scholarships — https://opportunity.collegeboard.org/home	**14** Check website for application: Elks Most Valuable Student Contest — www.elks.org/enf/scholars/mvs.cfm or contact your local Elks lodge	**15** Check website for Prudential Emerging Visionaries process (formerly Prudential Spirit of Community Award) — https://www.prudential.com/links/about/emergingvisionaries (OPEN TO STUDENTS AGES 14 TO 18)	**16** Are you a female currently studying engineering, engineering technology and computer science ? If yes, visit this page for many opportunities through the Society of Women Engineers — https://swe.org/scholarships or www.swe.org (see Scholarships)	**17** National YoungArts Foundation competition entry due — www.youngarts.org	**18** **Check website for ServiceNow Scholarship Program application — https://learn-more.scholarsapply.org/servicenow	**19** Check website for application: Burger King Scholars Program — https://www.burgerkingfoundation.org/ or https://burger-king.scholarsapply.org
20	**21** *Check website for Essential Visionaries Scholarship Fund - https://learn-more.scholarsapply.org/essentialvisionaries	**22** **Check website for nomination process — All-USA Community College Academic Team — www.ptk.org (see Scholarships)	**23** Check website for FRA Foundation Scholarship applications —www.fra.org (see Events and Programs < Education Foundation Scholarships) (OPEN TO STUDENT FRA MEMBERS AFFILIATED WITH THE U.S. NAVY, MARINE CORPS OR COAST GUARD THEMSELVES OR THROUGH FAMILY MEMBER)	**24** Chick-fil-A Community Scholarship application due — https://www.chick-fil-a.com/communityscholars	**25** Marianne, $400,000 scholarship winner can take you step by step through the scholarship process in The Scholarship Boot Camp. Scan this QR code to learn more.	**26** Check website for rules: American Fire Sprinkler Association High School Seniors Scholarship Contest — www.afsascholarship.org
27 +Check website for iVein Health & Wellness Scholarship application —https://www.ivein.com/scholarship/	**28** Check website for entry rules: "Frame My Future" Scholarship Contest — www.framemyfuture.com or https://www.diplomaframe.com/contests/frame-my-future-scholarship.aspx	**29** VFW Voice of Democracy Audio Essay Contest deadline—OCTOBER 31 — https://www.vfw.org/community/youth-and-education/youth-scholarships (OPEN TO GRADES 9 THRU 12)	**30** VFW Patriot's Pen Essay Contest entries due OCTOBER 31— https://www.vfw.org/community/youth-and-education/youth-scholarships (OPEN TO GRADES 6 THRU 8)	**31** National Security Agency Stokes Educational Scholarship Program application due — https://www.intelligencecareers.gov/NSA/students-and-internships STOKES MAY BE OFFERED BY OTHER GOVERNMENT AGENCIES.		

Copyright © 2024
The Scholarship Workshop LLC • P. O. Box 176 • Centreville, Virginia 20122 • www.scholarshipworkshop.com

The Scholarship Monthly Planner

Notes

_____
_____
_____
_____
_____
_____
_____
_____
_____
_____
_____
_____
_____
_____
_____
_____
_____
_____
_____
_____
_____
_____
_____
_____
_____

DON'T FORGET!

- Final deadline dates have red text.
- Submit your application at least 7 days before the deadline.
- Always look at least 1 month ahead to get prepared for upcoming deadlines.
- Hate writing? Start on your essay at least 1 month prior to the deadline.
- Need recommendations? Ask at least 4 weeks prior to the deadline. Follow-up! Also, many programs request recommendations electronically. Please let someone know you've provided their e-mail address for a recommendation, so they will be prepared for the e-mail request.
- As you download applications, organize them. You should have one folder for each month. Place applications in the appropriate folder for each month. For example, all applications that are due in December should be in a folder marked December.
- Check previous months for application download dates or activities you need to complete. These activities are shown in black text. Although you may be behind with some activities, the deadline date for a scholarship or award may not have passed.
- Research and include local, regional, and state based scholarships in your calendar.
- Research and include scholarships based on your interests, personal characteristics, and situation in your calendar.
- Request nominations with a letter and your résumé.

Copyright © 2024
The Scholarship Workshop LLC • P. O. Box 176 • Centreville, Virginia 20122 • www.scholarshipworkshop.com

The Scholarship Monthly Planner
November 2024

*Programs are open to current college students and <u>and</u> high school seniors.

**Programs are open to current college students only.

***Programs are open to graduate and/or professional school students only.

+Program open to graduate and undergraduate students

Unless otherwise noted, all other programs are open to high school seniors.

SUN	MON	TUE	WED	THU	FRI	SAT
+Check website for Alpha Kappa Alpha Educational Advancement Scholarship application — www.akaeaf.org	***Contact your medical school's dean, student affairs or financial aid office to be considered for an AMA Foundation Physicians of Tomorrow Scholarship nomination —https:// amafoundation.org/ programs/scholarships	Check website for application: Jackie Robinson Scholarship Program — www.jackierobinson.org	**Check website for Coupons Plus Deals Scholarship—https:// www.couponsplusdeals.com/scholarship (OPEN TO 3RD OR 4TH YEAR COLLEGE STUDENTS)	**1** Prudential Emerging Visionaries entries due soon (formerly Prudential Spirit of Community Award) — https:// www.prudential.com/ links/about/ emergingvisionaries (OPEN TO STUDENTS AGES 14 TO 18)	**1** Check website for Dell Scholarship Program application — www.dellscholars.org	**2** Check website for NHS Scholarship program application — www.nhs.us/scholarship
3 *+Check website for William A. March Education Trust Scholarship — https:// learn-more.scholarsapply.org/ williammarchscholarship	**4** **Check website for Wellroot Family Services Scholarship Program application — https:// learn-more.scholarsapply.org/wellrootscholarship	**5** Check website for Stockholm Junior Water Prize state competition entry forms — www.wef.org/SJWP/ (OPEN TO GRADES 9 THRU 12)	**6** ***GEM fellowship application due NOVEMBER 8 — www.gemfellowship.org	**7** Regeneron Science Talent Search entry due — www.societyforscience.org/sts or student.societyforscience.org/regeneron-sts	**8** **TE Connectivity African Heritage Scholarship Program application due — https:// learn-more.scholarsapply.org/ teconnectivity-african-heritage/	**9** Check website for Ron Brown Scholarship application — www.ronbrown.org
10 Check website for application: DEWALT Trades Scholarship — https:// learn-more.scholarsapply.org/dewalttrade/ (OPEN TO STUDENTS ATTENDING TWO-YEAR COLLEGE OR VOCATIONAL-TECHNICAL SCHOOLS) *1000 APPLICATION LIMIT. APPLY EARLY.*	**11** *Check website for Essential Visionaries Scholarship Fund - https:// learn-more.scholarsapply.org/essentialvisionaries	**12** Elks Most Valuable Student application due — www.elks.org/enf/scholars/	**13** If you're in NHS, confirm National Honor Society Scholarship Program verification process and deadline — www.nhs.us/ scholarship	**14** Check website for GE–Reagan Foundation Scholarship Program application — www.reaganfoundation.org/ge-rfscholarships.aspx Facebook page: https:// www.facebook.com/ GEReaganScholarships	**15** Soroptimist Live Your Dream Awards application due — https:// www.soroptimist.org/our-work/live-your-dream-awards (OPEN TO WOMEN WHO ARE PRIMARY FINANCIAL SUPPORT FOR THEIR HOUSEHOLD)	**16** Jack Kent Cooke College Scholarship Program application due — https:// www.jkcf.org/our-scholarships/college-scholarship-program/
17 *Check website for Create-A-Greeting-Card Scholarship Contest entry rules — www.gallerycollection.com/ greetingcardscontests.htm (OPEN TO NONTRADITIONAL STUDENTS)	**18** *Check website for Taco Bell Live Mas Scholarship — https:// www.tacobellfoundation.org/live-mas-scholarship/ (OPEN TO STUDENTS AGE 16 TO 26)	**19** Check website for SkyWater Foundation Scholarship application — https:// learn-more.scholarsapply.org/ skywater APPLY EARLY. ONLY FIRST 1000 APPLICATIONS ACCEPTED.	**20** Check website:: Amazon Future Engineer Scholarship application — https:// scholarshipamerica.org/ amazonfutureengineer/	**21** Check website for application: Jeanette Rankin Scholar Grant — www.rankinfoundation.org (OPEN TO WOMEN 35+)	**22** Check out College Board Opportunity Scholarships — https:// opportunity.collegeboard.org/home	**23** Check website for American Water Inclusion and Diversity Scholarship — https:// learn-more.scholarsapply.org/ american-water
24 +Check website for Progress of Ideas Scholarship application — https:// learn-more.scholarsapply.org/schalkenbach/	**25** **Check website for Ritchie-Jennings Memorial Scholarship application — www.acfe.com/ scholarship.aspx	**26** Check website for TheDream.US National Scholarship Program application — https:// www.thedream.us (FOR DREAMERS/DACA STUDENTS)	**27** If you haven't already, start working on your Free application for Federal Student Aid (FAFSA) —www.fafsa.ed.gov Also contact schools and states for their specific deadlines.	**28** Check website: American Foreign Service Essay Contest entry rules — www.afsa.org/ essaycontest/	**29** ServiceNow Scholarship Program application due — https:// learn-more.scholarsapply.org/ servicenow	**30** Check website for the Anne Ford Scholarship application — www.ncld.org Check website for the Allegra Ford Thomas Scholarship application — www.ncld.org

The Scholarship Monthly Planner

Notes

DON'T FORGET!

- Final deadline dates have red text.
- Submit your application at least 7 days before the deadline.
- Always look at least 1 month ahead to get prepared for upcoming deadlines.
- Hate writing? Start on your essay at least 1 month prior to the deadline.
- Need recommendations? Ask at least 4 weeks prior to the deadline. Follow-up! Also, many programs request recommendations electronically. Please let someone know you've provided their e-mail address for a recommendation, so they will be prepared for the e-mail request.
- As you download applications, organize them. You should have one folder for each month. Place applications in the appropriate folder for each month. For example, all applications that are due in December should be in a folder marked December.
- Check previous months for application download dates or activities you need to complete. These activities are shown in black text. Although you may be behind with some activities, the deadline date for a scholarship or award may not have passed.
- Research and include local, regional, and state based scholarships in your calendar.
- Research and include scholarships based on your interests, personal characteristics, and situation in your calendar.
- Request nominations with a letter and your résumé.

Copyright © 2024
The Scholarship Workshop LLC • P. O. Box 176 • Centreville, Virginia 20122 • www.scholarshipworkshop.com

The Scholarship Monthly Planner

December 2024

*Programs are open to current college students and high school seniors.

**Programs are open to current college students only.

***Programs are open to graduate and/or professional school students only.

+Program open to graduate and undergraduate students

Unless otherwise noted, all other programs are open to high school seniors.

SUN	MON	TUE	WED	THU	FRI	SAT
				**Request application due date for Coca-Cola Community College Academic Team nomination team at your institution — www.ptk.org (see Scholarships)	+The Christophers Annual Video Contest entry due soon — https://www.christophers.org/video-contest-for-college-students or https://www.christophers.org	Americanism Essay Contest entries due DECEMBER 1 — www.fra.org (see Events and Program < Americanism Essay Contest) (OPEN TO GRADES 7 THRU 12)
1 Ron Brown Scholar application due — www.ronbrown.org ——— Dell Scholarship Program application due DECEMBER 1 — www.dellscholars.org	**2** Check website for SNC Women in STEM Scholarship application — https://learn-more.scholarsapply.org/snc/	**3** Check website for The George S. & Stella M. Knight Essay Contest information and rules — www.sar.org (see Education) (OPEN TO GRADES 9 THRU 12)	**4** Check website for Mu Alpha Theta Scholarships — www.mualphatheta.org	**5** +*Stop Hunger Scholarship Program deadline — www.sodexofoundation.org or http://us.stop-hunger.org/home/grants.html (OPEN TO STUDENTS IN KINDERGARTEN THROUGH GRADUATE SCHOOL)	**6** *+Ronald V. Dellums Memorial SMART Scholarship application due — https://www.smartscholarship.org/smart ——— +SMART Scholarship Program application due — https://www.smartscholarship.org/smart	**7** Contact your local Executive Women International chapter for information on Adult Students in Scholastic Transition scholarship process — www.ewiconnect.com (OPEN TO ADULT STUDENTS)
8 *Check website for Dunkin' Baltimore/Metro DC Regional Scholarship — https://learn-more.scholarsapply.org/dunkinbaltimoredc	**9** *Check website for application: Hispanic Scholarship Fund — www.hsf.net	**10** Optimist International Essay and Oratorical Contests deadline in late December (contact local club for specific dates) — www.optimist.org/e/member/scholarships1.cfm# (OPEN TO STUDENTS UNDER AGE 19 AS OF 10/1/2024)	**11** **Wellroot Family Services Scholarship Program application due — https://learn-more.scholarsapply.org/wellrootscholarship/	**12** Check website for SkyWater Foundation Scholarship application — https://learn-more.scholarsapply.org/skywater APPLY EARLY. ONLY FIRST 1000 APPLICATIONS ACCEPTED.	**13** Burger King Scholars Program application due — https://www.burgerkingfoundation.org	**14** Contact your local Optimist Club for information about the Optimist International Essay and Oratorical Contests — www.optimist.org or https://www.optimist.org/member/scholarships1.cfm (OPEN TO STUDENTS UNDER AGE 19)
15 Equitable Excellence Scholarship application due DECEMBER 16 (there may be an application limit so apply early)— https://equitable.com/foundation/equitable-excellence-scholarship	**16** Amazon Future Engineer Scholarship application due https://scholarshipamerica.org/amazonfutureengineer/	**17** Check website for The Joseph S. Rumbaugh Historical Oration Contest information and rules — www.sar.org (see Education) (OPEN TO GRADES 9 THRU 12)	**18** Check website for DECA Scholarship Program application — www.deca.org/scholarships	**19** Check website for rules: American Fire Sprinkler Association High School Senior Scholarship Contest — www.afsascholarship.org	**20** Use the *Federal Student Aid Estimator* to get an early estimate of your eligibility for federal student aid — https://studentaid.gov/aid-estimator/	**21**
22 Check website for Arthur M. & Berdena King Eagle Scout Contest rules — www.sar.org (see Education)	**23** Check website for Simon Youth Foundation Scholarship application — https://syf.org/scholarships/ Also see https://www.facebook.com/simonyouthfoundation or https://twitter.com/simon_youth	**24** Check out College Board Opportunity Scholarships — https://opportunity.collegeboard.org/home	**25** +Check website for application: Military Spouse Scholarships — https://www.militaryfamily.org/programs/spouses-scholarships/ (OPEN TO NONTRADITIONAL STUDENTS)	**26** Check out the Horatio Alger National Scholarship Application — www.horatioalger.org or https://scholars.horatioalger.org (OPEN TO HIGH SCHOOL JUNIORS)	**27** Check website for application: Scholarships for Military Children — www.militaryscholar.org or https://fisherhouse.org/programs/scholarship-programs	**28** **Check website for Scholarship America Dream Award Application — https://scholarshipamerica.org/students/browse-scholarships/apply-for-the-dream-award
29 +iVein Health & Wellness Scholarship application due — https://www.ivein.com/scholarship/	**30** Unigo $10,000 Scholarship entry due DECEMBER 31 — https://www.unigo.com/scholarships/our-scholarships/unigo-10k-scholarship	**31** **Deadline for Coupons Plus Deals Scholarship—https://www.couponsplusdeals.com/scholarship (OPEN TO 3RD OR 4TH YEAR COLLEGE STUDENTS)				

Copyright © 2024

The Scholarship Workshop LLC • P. O. Box 176 • Centreville, Virginia 20122 • www.scholarshipworkshop.com

The Scholarship Monthly Planner

Notes

_____

_____

_____

_____

_____

_____

_____

_____

_____

_____

_____

_____

_____

_____

_____

_____

_____

_____

_____

_____

_____

_____

DON'T FORGET!

- Final deadline dates have red text.
- Submit your application at least 7 days before the deadline.
- Always look at least 1 month ahead to get prepared for upcoming deadlines.
- Hate writing? Start on your essay at least 1 month prior to the deadline.
- Need recommendations? Ask at least 4 weeks prior to the deadline. Follow-up! Also, many programs request recommendations electronically. Please let someone know you've provided their e-mail address for a recommendation, so they will be prepared for the e-mail request.
- As you download applications, organize them. You should have one folder for each month. Place applications in the appropriate folder for each month. For example, all applications that are due in December should be in a folder marked December.
- Check previous months for application download dates or activities you need to complete. These activities are shown in black text. Although you may be behind with some activities, the deadline date for a scholarship or award may not have passed.
- Research and include local, regional, and state based scholarships in your calendar.
- Research and include scholarships based on your interests, personal characteristics, and situation in your calendar.
- Request nominations with a letter and your résumé.

Copyright © 2024
The Scholarship Workshop LLC • P. O. Box 176 • Centreville, Virginia 20122 • www.scholarshipworkshop.com

The Scholarship Monthly Planner
January 2025

*Programs are open to current college students and high school seniors.

**Programs are open to current college students only.

***Programs are open to graduate and/or professional school students only.

+Program open to graduate and undergraduate students

Unless otherwise noted, all other programs are open to high school seniors.

SUN	MON	TUE	WED	THU	FRI	SAT
			*Check website for Orphan Foundation of America Foster Care to Success scholarship application — https://www.fc2success.org/programs/scholarships-and-grants/	Check website for Mu Alpha Theta Scholarships — www.mualphatheta.org	Check website for Northwestern Mutual Childhood Cancer Survivor and Sibling Scholarship applications — https://learn-more.scholarsapply.org/nmsurvivors/	Contact the National Society of the Daughters of the American Revolution (NSDAR) for information about their scholarship programs — www.dar.org or https://dar.academicworks.com
National Beta Club scholarship application due soon — www.betaclub.org/scholarship	Check website for Cameron Impact Scholarship — https://www.bryancameroneducationfoundation.org This scholarship has an application limit. Apply early.	Check website for application: Hispanic Scholarship Fund — www.hsf.net	1 American Fire Sprinkler Association High School Senior Scholarship entry due — www.afsascholarship.org Also see @afsascholarship and www.facebook.com/afsascholarship/	2 GE–Reagan Foundation Scholarship Program application deadline soon — www.reaganfoundation.org/ge-rfscholarships.aspx or https://www.facebook.com/GEReaganScholarships	3 **Check website for Wells Fargo Veterans Scholarship program application—https://learn-more.scholarsapply.org/wellsfargoveterans/	4 + Check website for Wireless History Foundation Scholarship application — https://learn-more.scholarsapply.org/whf/
5 *Check website for 100 Black Men Scholarship— www.100blackmen.org or https://100blackmen.org/program-activations/annual-scholarship-program or contact a local chapter	6 Contact your local Executive Women International chapter for information on EWISP scholarship process — www.ewiconnect.com	7 Check website for application: Jeanette Rankin Scholar Grant — www.rankinfoundation.org (OPEN TO WOMEN 35+)	8 *+William A. March Education Trust Scholarship application due — https://learn-more.scholarsapply.org/williammarchscholarship	9 *Check website for Steiner Family Scholarship — https://learn-more.scholarsapply.org/steinerfamilyscholarship (OPEN TO STUDENTS IN US AND CANADA)	10 Jackie Robinson scholarship application due — www.jackierobinson.org	11 **Jack Kent Cooke Undergraduate Transfer Scholarship application due — www.jkcf.org
12 DECA Scholarship Program application due — www.deca.org/scholarships	13 If you haven't already, start working on your Free application for Federal Student Aid (FAFSA) — https://studentaid.gov Contact schools and states for their specific deadlines..	14 *SNC Women in STEM Scholarship application due — https://learn-more.scholarsapply.org/snc/	15 *Check website for Lockheed Martin STEM Scholarship application — www.lockheedmartin.com/scholarship	16 *Essential Visionaries Scholarship Fund application due - https://learn-more.scholarsapply.org/essentialvisionaries	17 John F. Kennedy Profile in Courage Essay Contest entry due — www.jfklibrary.org/ (OPEN TO GRADES 9 THRU 12)	18 Check website for Lockheed Martin Vocational Scholarship application — https://lockheedmartin.com/en-us/who-we-are/communities/stem-education/lockheed-martin-vocational-scholarship.html
19 Check website for Doodle 4 Google entry rules and deadline— www.google.com/doodle4google (OPEN TO STUDENTS IN KINDERGARTEN THRU 12)	20 C-Span's StudentCam competition deadline — http://www.studentcam.org (OPEN TO STUDENTS IN GRADES 6 THRU 12)	21 Check website: Dr. Arnita Young Boswell Scholarship — www.nhbwinc.com or https://nhbwinc.org/scholarships	22 Check website for Jack Kent Cooke Young Scholars Program application — https://www.jkcf.org/our-scholarships/young-scholars-program/ (OPEN TO 7TH GRADE STUDENTS ONLY)	23 *Taco Bell Live Mas Scholarship submission due soon — https://www.tacobellfoundation.org/live-mas-scholarship/ (OPEN TO STUDENTS AGE 16 TO 26)	24 *+Check website for Dr. Angela E. Grant Memorial Scholarship deadline—http://drangelagrantscholarship.org (OPEN TO CANCER SURVIVORS OR THOSE WITH IMMEDIATE FAMILY MEMBERS DIAGNOSED WITH CANCER)	25 Check out College Board Opportunity Scholarships — https://opportunity.collegeboard.org/home
26 Check website for Gloria Barron Prize for Young Heroes application — https://barronprize.org/apply (OPEN TO STUDENTS AGE 8 TO 18)	27	28 Toshiba NSTA ExploraVision Awards application due JANUARY 31 — www.exploravision.org (OPEN TO STUDENTS IN GRADES K—12)	29 +Progress of Ideas Scholarship application due JANUARY 31 — https://learn-more.scholarsapply.org/schalkenbach/	30 National Society of the Daughters of the American Revolution (NSDAR) scholarship application due JANUARY 31 — www.dar.org or https://dar.academicworks.com	31 American Water Inclusion and Diversity Scholarship application due — https://learn-more.scholarsapply.org/american-water	

Copyright © 2024
The Scholarship Workshop LLC • P. O. Box 176 • Centreville, Virginia 20122 • www.scholarshipworkshop.com

The Scholarship Monthly Planner

Notes

_____
_____
_____
_____
_____
_____
_____
_____
_____
_____
_____
_____
_____
_____
_____
_____
_____
_____
_____
_____
_____
_____
_____
_____

DON'T FORGET!

- Final deadline dates have red text.
- Submit your application at least 7 days before the deadline.
- Always look at least 1 month ahead to get prepared for upcoming deadlines.
- Hate writing? Start on your essay at least 1 month prior to the deadline.
- Need recommendations? Ask at least 4 weeks prior to the deadline. Follow-up! Also, many programs request recommendations electronically. Please let someone know you've provided their e-mail address for a recommendation, so they will be prepared for the e-mail request.
- As you download applications, organize them. You should have one folder for each month. Place applications in the appropriate folder for each month. For example, all applications that are due in December should be in a folder marked December.
- Check previous months for application download dates or activities you need to complete. These activities are shown in black text. Although you may be behind with some activities, the deadline date for a scholarship or award may not have passed.
- Research and include local, regional, and state based scholarships in your calendar.
- Research and include scholarships based on your interests, personal characteristics, and situation in your calendar.
- Request nominations with a letter and your résumé.

Copyright © 2024
The Scholarship Workshop LLC • P. O. Box 176 • Centreville, Virginia 20122 • www.scholarshipworkshop.com

The Scholarship Monthly Planner
February 2025

*Programs are open to current college students and high school seniors.

**Programs are open to current college students only.

***Programs are open to graduate and/or professional school students only.

+Program open to graduate and undergraduate students

Unless otherwise noted, all other programs are open to high school seniors.

SUN	MON	TUE	WED	THU	FRI	SAT
					Check website for BHW Women in STEM Scholarship application—https://thebhwgroup.com/scholarship (ALSO OPEN TO INTERNATIONAL STUDENTS)	**1** *Mu Alpha Theta Scholarship application due FEBRUARY 1 — www.mualphatheta.org
2 The Christophers Annual Poster Contest deadline this month — https://www.christophers.org/poster-contest or https://www.christophers.org	**3** Northwestern Mutual Childhood Cancer Survivor and Sibling Scholarship application due — https://learnmore.scholarsapply.org/nmsurvivors/	**4** Entry due soon for Davidson Fellows Scholarship application process — http://www.davidsongifted.org/Fellows-Scholarship (OPEN TO ALL STUDENTS UNDER AGE 18)	**5** George S. & Stella M. Knight Essay Contest deadline soon — www.sar.org	**6** American Foreign Service Essay Contest entry due soon — www.afsa.org/essaycontest/	**7** **Ritchie-Jennings Memorial Scholarship application due — www.acfe.com/scholarship.aspx	**8** +Check website for International Bridge, Tunnel and Turnpike Association Scholarship Program application — https://www.ibtta.org/ibtta-foundation-scholarship-program
9 Begin working on Ayn Rand "Anthem" Essay Contest entry or https://aynrand.org/students/essay-contests (OPEN TO GRADES 8 THRU 12)	**10** Check website for Horatio Alger Career & Technical Scholarship Program Application — www.horatioalger.org or https://scholars.horatioalger.org (MUST BE HIGH SCHOOL GRADUATE ENROLLED IN AN ASSOCIATE'S DEGREE, CERTIFICATE, OR DIPLOMA PROGRAM)	**11** Simon Youth Foundation Scholarship application due soon — https://syf.org/scholarships/ Also see https://www.facebook.com/simonyouthfoundation or https://twitter.com/simon_youth	**12** Scholarships for Military Children application due FEBRUARY 15 — https://militaryscholar.org or https://fisherhouse.org/programs/scholarship-programs	**13** Google Lime Scholarship deadline soon — https://www.limeconnect.com/programs/page/google-lime-scholarship (OPEN TO STUDENTS WITH DISABILITIES)	**14** Check website for Scholarship America Barry Griswell Scholarship — https://learnmore.scholarsapply.org/barrygriswellscholarship/ (ALSO OPEN TO NON-TRADITIONAL STUDENTS)	**15** *+Hispanic Scholarship Fund application due — www.hsf.net
16 Jeanette Rankin Women's Scholarship Fund application due — www.rankinfoundation.org (OPEN TO WOMEN 35 AND UP)	**17** *Check website for Central Intelligence Agency (CIA) **Undergraduate** Scholarship Program application — https://www.cia.gov/careers/student-programs/	**18** ***Check website for Central Intelligence Agency (CIA) **Graduate Studies** Scholarship Program application — https://www.cia.gov/careers/student-programs/	**19** **Check website—National Association for Campus Activities for scholarship opportunities — https://www.naca.org/FOUNDATION/Pages/Scholarships.aspx	**20** **Check website for The Voyager Scholarship, The Obama-Chesky Scholarship for Public Service application — https://www.obama.org/voyager-scholarship/	**21** Check website for Super Power Scholarship — https://www.unigo.com/scholarships/our-scholarships/superpower-scholarship (OPEN TO STUDENTS AGE 14 AND UP)	**22** **Check website for Scholarship America Dream Award Application — https://scholarshipamerica.org/students/browse-scholarships/apply-for-the-dream-award
23 *Check website for Varicent EDGE Scholarship application — https://learnmore.scholarsapply.org/varicentedge/ or https://www.varicent.com/company/edge-scholarship (APPLICATION LIMIT OF 500. APPLY EARLY!)	**24** TheDream.US National Scholarship Program application due soon— https://www.thedream.us (FOR DREAMERS/DACA STUDENTS)	**25** Check website for Jack Kent Cooke Young Scholars Program application — https://www.jkcf.org/our-scholarships/young-scholars-program/ (OPEN TO 7TH GRADE STUDENTS ONLY)	**26**	**27** Check website for Doodle 4 Google entry rules —www.google.com/doodle4google (OPEN TO STUDENTS IN KINDERGARTEN THRU 12)	**28** *Check website for Dunkin' Baltimore/Metro DC Regional Scholarship — https://learnmore.scholarsapply.org/dunkinbaltimoredc	

Copyright © 2024
The Scholarship Workshop LLC • P. O. Box 176 • Centreville, Virginia 20122 • www.scholarshipworkshop.com

The Scholarship Monthly Planner

Notes

- Final deadline dates have red text.
- Submit your application at least 7 days before the deadline.
- Always look at least 1 month ahead to get prepared for upcoming deadlines.
- Hate writing? Start on your essay at least 1 month prior to the deadline.
- Need recommendations? Ask at least 4 weeks prior to the deadline. Follow-up! Also, many programs request recommendations electronically. Please let someone know you've provided their e-mail address for a recommendation, so they will be prepared for the e-mail request.
- As you download applications, organize them. You should have one folder for each month. Place applications in the appropriate folder for each month. For example, all applications that are due in December should be in a folder marked December.
- Check previous months for application download dates or activities you need to complete. These activities are shown in black text. Although you may be behind with some activities, the deadline date for a scholarship or award may not have passed.
- Research and include local, regional, and state based scholarships in your calendar.
- Research and include scholarships based on your interests, personal characteristics, and situation in your calendar.
- Request nominations with a letter and your résumé.

Copyright © 2024
The Scholarship Workshop LLC • P. O. Box 176 • Centreville, Virginia 20122 • www.scholarshipworkshop.com

The Scholarship Monthly Planner
March 2025

*Programs are open to current college students and high school seniors.

**Programs are open to current college students only.

***Programs are open to graduate and/or professional school students only.

+Program open to graduate and undergraduate students

Unless otherwise noted, all other programs are open to high school seniors.

SUN	MON	TUE	WED	THU	FRI	SAT
		Begin looking for local scholarship and award opportunities. Many may have deadlines in this month or later. To learn more about finding local opportunities, see the chapter, "The Local Scholarship Search: Finding Scholarships in Your Backyard" in *Winning Scholarships for College*, 5th or later edition.	*Check website for Varicent EDGE Scholarship application — https://learn-more.scholarsapply.org/varicentedge/ or https://www.varicent.com/company/edge-scholarship	Check for various Ayn Rand Essay Contest deadlines — www.aynrand.org or www.aynrand.org/students/essay-contests (OPEN TO STUDENTS AGE 13+ INCLUDING COLLEGE STUDENTS, AND GRADUATE STUDENTS)	American Association on Health & Disability Scholarship Program application due MARCH 1 — https://www.aahd.us/initiatives/scholarship-program/ (OPEN TO STUDENTS WITH DISABILITIES)	**1** Leading the Future II Scholarship application due — www.scholarshipworkshop.com
2 Steiner Family Scholarship application due MARCH 3 — https://learn-more.scholarsapply.org/steinerfamilyscholarship (OPEN TO STUDENTS IN US AND CANADA)	**3** *Create-A-Greeting-Card Scholarship Contest entry due — www.gallerycollection.com/greetingcardscontests.htm (OPEN TO NONTRADITIONAL and INTERNATIONAL STUDENTS)	**4** Begin working on Ayn Rand "The Fountainhead" Essay Contest entry — www.aynrand.org (OPEN TO MIDDLE AND HIGH SCHOOL STUDENTS AGE 13 AND OLDER)	**5** Check website for Ruth Lilly and Dorothy Sargent Rosenberg Poetry Fellowships — www.poetryfoundation.org/foundation/prizes_fellowship (OPEN TO NONTRADITIONAL STUDENTS)	**6**	**7** Doodle 4 Google entry due soon — www.google.com/doodle4google (OPEN TO STUDENTS IN KINDERGARTEN THRU 12)	**8** Check website for Military Commanders' Scholarship application — https://learn-more.scholarsapply.org/militarycommanders or www.militarycommandersscholarship.org
9 "Frame My Future" Scholarship Contest deadline soon — www.framemyfuture.com or https://www.diplomaframe.com/contests/frame-my-future-scholarship.aspx	**10** **Complete Wells Fargo Veterans Scholarship application — https://learn-more.scholarsapply.org/wellsfargoveterans/ (APPLY EARLY. FUNDS CAN RUN OUT)	**11**	**12**	**13**	**14**	**15** Horatio Alger National Scholarship Application due — www.horatioalger.org or https://scholars.horatioalger.org (OPEN TO HIGH SCHOOL JUNIORS)
16 *Check website for Shawn Carter Scholarship — www.shawncartersf.com	**17** American Foreign Service Essay Contest entry due soon — www.afsa.org/essaycontest	**18**	**19**	**20** The Voyager Scholarship, The Obama-Chesky Scholarship for Public Service application due soon — https://www.obama.org/programs/voyager-scholarship/	**21** Start working on your outfit for the Stuck at Prom Contest — www.stuckatprom.com	**22**
23 Begin working on Ayn Rand "Anthem" Essay Contest entry or https://aynrand.org/students/essay-contests (OPEN TO GRADES 8 THRU 12)	**24**	**25** Anne Ford Scholarship application due soon — www.ncld.org (OPEN TO STUDENTS WITH LEARNING DISABILITIES) _____ Allegra Ford Thomas Scholarship application due soon— www.ncld.org (OPEN TO STUDENTS WITH LEARNING DISABILITIES)	**26** Lockheed Martin Vocational Scholarship application due soon — https://lockheedmartin.com/en-us/who-we-are/communities/stem-education/lockheed-martin-vocational-scholarship.html (OPEN TO STUDENTS PURSUING ASSOCIATE DEGREES OR CERTIFICATIONS)	**27** **Scholarship America Dream Award Application due — https://learn-more.scholarsapply.org/dreamaward/ _____ SkyWater Foundation Scholarship application due — https://learn-more.scholarsapply.org/skywater APPLY EARLY. ONLY FIRST 1000 APPLICATIONS ACCEPTED.	**28** ***Deadline for Beinecke Scholarship nomination — http://fdnweb.org/beinecke/ _____ +Wireless History Foundation Scholarship application due — https://learn-more.scholarsapply.org/whf/	**29** *Lockheed Martin STEM Scholarship application due soon — www.lockheedmartin.com/scholarship
30 Super Power Scholarship deadline MARCH 31 — https://www.unigo.com/scholarships/our-scholarships/superpower-scholarship	**31** *Orphan Foundation of America Foster Care to Success scholarship application due soon — https://www.fc2success.org/programs/scholarships-and-grants/					

Copyright © 2024
The Scholarship Workshop LLC • P. O. Box 176 • Centreville, Virginia 20122 • www.scholarshipworkshop.com

The Scholarship Monthly Planner

Notes

DON'T FORGET!

- Final deadline dates have red text.
- Submit your application at least 7 days before the deadline.
- Always look at least 1 month ahead to get prepared for upcoming deadlines.
- Hate writing? Start on your essay at least 1 month prior to the deadline.
- Need recommendations? Ask at least 4 weeks prior to the deadline. Follow-up! Also, many programs request recommendations electronically. Please let someone know you've provided their e-mail address for a recommendation, so they will be prepared for the e-mail request.
- As you download applications, organize them. You should have one folder for each month. Place applications in the appropriate folder for each month. For example, all applications that are due in December should be in a folder marked December.
- Check previous months for application download dates or activities you need to complete. These activities are shown in black text. Although you may be behind with some activities, the deadline date for a scholarship or award may not have passed.
- Research and include local, regional, and state based scholarships in your calendar.
- Research and include scholarships based on your interests, personal characteristics, and situation in your calendar.
- Request nominations with a letter and your résumé.

Copyright © 2024
The Scholarship Workshop LLC • P. O. Box 176 • Centreville, Virginia 20122 • www.scholarshipworkshop.com

The Scholarship Monthly Planner
April 2025

*Programs are open to current college students and high school seniors.

**Programs are open to current college students only.

***Programs are open to graduate and/or professional school students only.

+Program open to graduate and undergraduate students

Unless otherwise noted, all other programs are open to high school seniors.

SUN	MON	TUE	WED	THU	FRI	SAT
					National scholarship and award deadlines will decline significantly after this month. If you haven't already, begin intensive research for community and state based scholarships and awards. Consider reading *Last Minute College Financing Guide*.	Use this QR code to learn more about *Last Minute College Financing Guide*.
*Check website for Central Intelligence Agency (CIA) **Undergraduate** Scholarship Program application — https://www.cia.gov/careers/student-programs/	Submission deadline this month for Ruth Lilly and Dorothy Sargent Rosenberg Poetry Fellowships — www.poetryfoundation.org/foundation/prizes_fellowship (OPEN TO NONTRADITIONAL STUDENTS)	1 *Check website for Shawn Carter Scholarship — www.shawncartersf.com	2 *Check website for Pega Scholars Program application — https://learn-more.scholarsapply.org/pegascholars/ (APPLICATION LIMIT OF 150. APPLY EARLY. ALSO AVAILABLE TO INTERNATIONAL STUDENTS FROM CERTAIN COUNTRIES)	3 Check website for Horatio Alger Career & Technical Scholarship Program Application — www.horatioalger.org or https://scholars.horatioalger.org	4	5
6 ***Check website for Central Intelligence Agency (CIA) **Graduate** Scholarship Program application — https://www.cia.gov/careers/jobs/graduate-scholarship-program/	7 Check website for Do-Over Scholarship — https://www.unigo.com/scholarships/our-scholarships/do-over-scholarship (OPEN TO STUDENTS AGE 13 AND UP)	8	9	10 Check website for Cameron Impact Scholarship early deadline — https://www.bryancameroneducationfoundation.org This scholarship has an application limit so apply early!	11	12 BHW Women in STEM Scholarship application due APRIL 15 — https://thebhwgroup.com/scholarship
13 Stockholm Junior Water Prize state competition entries due APRIL 15 — www.wef.org/SJWP/ (OPEN TO GRADES 9 THRU 12)	14 FRA Foundation Scholarship applications due APRIL 15 — www.fra.org (see Events and Programs < Education Foundation Scholarships) (OPEN TO STUDENT FRA MEMBERS AFFILIATED WITH THE U.S. NAVY, MARINE CORPS OR COAST GUARD THEMSELVES OR THROUGH FAMILY MEMBER)	15 +Alpha Kappa Alpha Educational Advancement Scholarship applications due — www.akaeaf.org ——————— Gloria Barron Prize for Young Heroes application due APRIL 15— https://barronprize.org/apply (OPEN TO STUDENTS AGE 8 TO 18)	16 *Dunkin' Baltimore/Metro DC Regional Scholarship application due — https://learn-more.scholarsapply.org/dunkinbaltimoredc	17 +International Bridge, Tunnel and Turnpike Association Scholarship Program application due APRIL 18 — https://www.ibtta.org/ibtta-foundation-scholarship-program	18 Wells Fargo Scholarship Program for People with Disabilities application due — https://learn-more.scholarsapply.org/pwdscholarship/	19
20	21	22	23 Check website for Navisite's Next Steminist Scholarship Program — https://www.navisite.com/navisites-next-steminist/ (OPEN TO FEMALES 25 OR YOUNGER PURSUING STEM MAJORS)	24	25 Start working on your outfit for the Stuck at Prom Contest — www.stuckatprom.com	26
27	28	29 *Shawn Carter Scholarship application due APRIL 30 — www.shawncartersf.com Also see www.facebook.com/SCScholarship and www.twitter.com/ShawnCarterSF	30 *** Ragins/Braswell National Scholarship application due — www.scholarshipworkshop.com			

Copyright © 2024
The Scholarship Workshop LLC • P. O. Box 176 • Centreville, Virginia 20122 • www.scholarshipworkshop.com

The Scholarship Monthly Planner

Notes

DON'T FORGET!

- Final deadline dates have red text.
- Submit your application at least 7 days before the deadline.
- Always look at least 1 month ahead to get prepared for upcoming deadlines.
- Hate writing? Start on your essay at least 1 month prior to the deadline.
- Need recommendations? Ask at least 4 weeks prior to the deadline. Follow-up! Also, many programs request recommendations electronically. Please let someone know you've provided their e-mail address for a recommendation, so they will be prepared for the e-mail request.
- As you download applications, organize them. You should have one folder for each month. Place applications in the appropriate folder for each month. For example, all applications that are due in December should be in a folder marked December.
- Check previous months for application download dates or activities you need to complete. These activities are shown in black text. Although you may be behind with some activities, the deadline date for a scholarship or award may not have passed.
- Research and include local, regional, and state based scholarships in your calendar.
- Research and include scholarships based on your interests, personal characteristics, and situation in your calendar.
- Request nominations with a letter and your résumé.

Copyright © 2024
The Scholarship Workshop LLC • P. O. Box 176 • Centreville, Virginia 20122 • www.scholarshipworkshop.com

The Scholarship Monthly Planner
May 2025

*Programs are open to current college students and high school seniors.

**Programs are open to current college students only.

***Programs are open to graduate and/or professional school students only.

+Program open to graduate and undergraduate students

Unless otherwise noted, all other programs are open to high school seniors.

SUN	MON	TUE	WED	THU	FRI	SAT
	National scholarship and award deadlines usually decline in the late spring and summer. If you haven't already, begin intensive research for community and state based scholarships and awards. Consider reading *Last Minute College Financing Guide*.	Use this QR code to learn more about *Last Minute College Financing Guide*.	**Check website for application: Tylenol Future Care Scholarship Program — www.tylenol.com/news/subptyschol	**1** *+Dr. Angela E. Grant Memorial Scholarship deadline — http://drangelagrantscholarship.org (OPEN TO CANCER SURVIVORS OR THOSE WITH IMMEDIATE FAMILY MEMBERS DIAGNOSED WITH CANCER)	**2**	**3**
4	**5**	**6**	**7**	**8**	**9** Jack Kent Cooke Young Scholars Program application due — www.jkcf.org/scholarships (OPEN TO 7TH GRADE STUDENTS ONLY)	**10**
11	**12**	**13**	**14**	**15**	**16** Navisite's Next Steminist Scholarship application due soon — https://www.navisite.com/navisites-next-steminist/ (OPEN TO FEMALES 25 OR YOUNGER PURSUING STEM MAJORS)	**17** *+Check website for DoSomething.org Easy Scholarships — https://dosomething.org/pays-to-do-good or www.dosomething.org (*see Pays to Do Good*) This site has various scholarships with deadlines usually at the beginning or end of the month.
18	**19**	**20** Horatio Alger Career & Technical Scholarship Program Application due soon — https://scholars.horatioalger.org/about-our-scholarship-programs/technical/ (THIS IS A PRIORITY DEADLINE. YOU MAY BE ABLE TO SUBMIT AFTER THIS DATE IF ADDITIONAL FUNDS ARE AVAILABLE)	**21**	**22** *Scholarship America Barry Griswell Scholarship application due — https://learn-more.scholarsapply.org/barrygriswellscholarship (ALSO OPEN TO NON-TRADITIONAL STUDENTS)	**23** +Complete Military Spouse Scholarship application (awards made quarterly)— www.militaryfamily.org or https://www.militaryfamily.org/programs/spouses-scholarships/ (OPEN TO NONTRADITIONAL STUDENTS)	**24**
25	**26**	**27**	**28**	**29**	**30**	**31**

Copyright © 2024
The Scholarship Workshop LLC • P. O. Box 176 • Centreville, Virginia 20122 • www.scholarshipworkshop.com

The Scholarship Monthly Planner

Notes

_____

_____

_____

_____

_____

_____

_____

_____

_____

_____

_____

_____

_____

_____

_____

_____

_____

_____

_____

_____

_____

_____

_____

_____

_____

DON'T FORGET!

- Final deadline dates have red text.
- Submit your application at least 7 days before the deadline.
- Always look at least 1 month ahead to get prepared for upcoming deadlines.
- Hate writing? Start on your essay at least 1 month prior to the deadline.
- Need recommendations? Ask at least 4 weeks prior to the deadline. Follow-up! Also, many programs request recommendations electronically. Please let someone know you've provided their e-mail address for a recommendation, so they will be prepared for the e-mail request.
- As you download applications, organize them. You should have one folder for each month. Place applications in the appropriate folder for each month. For example, all applications that are due in December should be in a folder marked December.
- Check previous months for application download dates or activities you need to complete. These activities are shown in black text. Although you may be behind with some activities, the deadline date for a scholarship or award may not have passed.
- Research and include local, regional, and state based scholarships in your calendar.
- Research and include scholarships based on your interests, personal characteristics, and situation in your calendar.
- Request nominations with a letter and your résumé.

Copyright © 2024
The Scholarship Workshop LLC • P. O. Box 176 • Centreville, Virginia 20122 • www.scholarshipworkshop.com

The Scholarship Monthly Planner

June 2025

*Programs are open to current college students and high school seniors.

**Programs are open to current college students only.

***Programs are open to graduate and/or professional school students only.

+Program open to graduate and undergraduate students

Unless otherwise noted, all other programs are open to high school seniors.

SUN	MON	TUE	WED	THU	FRI	SAT
	National scholarship and award deadlines usually decline in the late spring and summer. If you haven't already, begin intensive research for community and state based scholarships and awards. Consider reading *Last Minute College Financing Guide.*		IF YOU JUST STARTED USING THIS EDITION OF *THE SCHOLARSHIP MONTHLY PLANNER,* WE HAVE A PREPUBLICATION DISCOUNT ON *THE SCHOLARSHIP MONTHLY PLANNER* FOR THE **2025-2026 ACADEMIC YEAR DUE IN AUGUST 2025**, PLEASE CONTACT THE SCHOLARSHIP WORKSHOP AT info@scholarshipworkshop.com for more details.			******Begin work on Platt Family Scholarship Prize Essay Contest entry — https://www.thelincolnforum.org/platt-family-essay-contest (OPEN TO FULL-TIME, UNDERGRADUATE STUDENTS IN AN AMERICAN COLLEGE OR UNIVERSITY. US CITIZENSHIP IS NOT REQUIRED.)
1 Stuck at Prom Contest entries due this month — www.stuckatprom.com Check website for official rules.	**2**	**3**	**4** **Check website—National Association for Campus Activities for scholarship opportunities—https://www.naca.org/FOUNDATION/Pages/Scholarships.aspx	**5**	**6** **Check website for application: Tylenol Future Care Scholarship Program — www.tylenol.com/news/subptyschol	**7**
8	**9**	**10**	**11**	**12**	**13** ***Central Intelligence Agency (CIA) Graduate Studies Scholarship Program application due soon — https://www.cia.gov/careers/student-programs/	**14** *Central Intelligence Agency (CIA) Undergraduate Scholarship Program application due soon — https://www.cia.gov/careers/student-programs/
15	**16**	**17**	**18**	**19**	**20** *+Check website for DoSomething.org Easy Scholarships — https://dosomething.org/pays-to-do-good or www.dosomething.org *(see Pays to Do Good)* This site has various scholarships with deadlines usually at the beginning or end of the month.	**21**
22	**23**	**24**	**25**	**26**	**27**	**28**
29	**30** Do-Over Scholarship deadline — https://www.unigo.com/scholarships/our-scholarships/do-over-scholarship (OPEN TO STUDENTS AGE 14 AND UP)					

Copyright © 2024
The Scholarship Workshop LLC • P. O. Box 176 • Centreville, Virginia 20122 • www.scholarshipworkshop.com

The Scholarship Monthly Planner

Notes

_____
_____
_____
_____
_____
_____
_____
_____
_____
_____
_____
_____
_____
_____
_____
_____
_____
_____
_____
_____
_____
_____
_____
_____
_____
_____
_____

DON'T FORGET!

- Final deadline dates have red text.
- Submit your application at least 7 days before the deadline.
- Always look at least 1 month ahead to get prepared for upcoming deadlines.
- Hate writing? Start on your essay at least 1 month prior to the deadline.
- Need recommendations? Ask at least 4 weeks prior to the deadline. Follow-up! Also, many programs request recommendations electronically. Please let someone know you've provided their e-mail address for a recommendation, so they will be prepared for the e-mail request.
- As you download applications, organize them. You should have one folder for each month. Place applications in the appropriate folder for each month. For example, all applications that are due in December should be in a folder marked December.
- Check previous months for application download dates or activities you need to complete. These activities are shown in black text. Although you may be behind with some activities, the deadline date for a scholarship or award may not have passed.
- Research and include local, regional, and state based scholarships in your calendar.
- Research and include scholarships based on your interests, personal characteristics, and situation in your calendar.
- Request nominations with a letter and your résumé.

Copyright © 2024
The Scholarship Workshop LLC • P. O. Box 176 • Centreville, Virginia 20122 • www.scholarshipworkshop.com

The Scholarship Monthly Planner

July 2025

*Programs are open to current college students and high school seniors.

**Programs are open to current college students only.

***Programs are open to graduate and/or professional school students only.

+Program open to graduate and undergraduate students

Unless otherwise noted, all other programs are open to high school seniors.

SUN	MON	TUE	WED	THU	FRI	SAT
National scholarship and award deadlines usually decline in the late spring and summer. If you haven't already, begin intensive research for community and state based scholarships and awards. Consider reading the *Last Minute College Financing Guide.*	Use this QR code to learn more about *Last Minute College Financing Guide.*		IF YOU JUST STARTED USING THIS EDITION OF *THE SCHOLARSHIP MONTHLY PLANNER,* WE HAVE A PREPUBLICATION DISCOUNT ON *THE SCHOLARSHIP MONTHLY PLANNER* FOR THE **2025-2026 ACADEMIC YEAR DUE IN AUGUST 2025.** PLEASE CONTACT THE SCHOLARSHIP WORKSHOP AT info@scholarshipworkshop.com for more details.	If you will be a college freshman in the upcoming academic year, get ready now for upcoming August deadlines and activities.	Check out *Scholarships for College Students* on Amazon. This book is helpful for rising college freshmen and current college students..	Current college students should research associations and organizations related to their major or minor for scholarship and award opportunities.
		1	**2** *+Check website for DoSomething.org Easy Scholarships — https://dosomething.org/pays-to-do-good or www.dosomething.org *(see Pays to Do Good)*	**3** Review *Scholarships for College Students* — a guide to help current college students find and win scholarship money.. See www.scholarshipworkshop.com/bookstore	**4**	**5**
6	**7**	**8**	**9** Graduate and professional school students should research government agencies and research oriented companies in need of individuals from their study area.	**10**	**11** * Pega Scholars Program application due — https://learn-more.scholarsapply.org/pegascholars/ (APPLICATION LIMIT OF 150. APPLY EARLY. ALSO AVAILABLE TO INTERNATIONAL STUDENTS FROM CERTAIN COUNTRIES)	**12**
13	**14**	**15**	**16**	**17** Tylenol Future Care Scholarship Program application due soon — www.tylenol.com/news/subptyschol	**18**	**19**
20	**21**	**22** *+Check website for DoSomething.org Easy Scholarships — https://dosomething.org/pays-to-do-good or www.dosomething.org *(see Pays to Do Good)* This site has various scholarships with deadlines usually at the beginning or end of the month.	**23**	**24**	**25**	**26**
27	**28**	**29**	**30**	**31** **Platt Family Scholarship Prize Essay Contest entry due soon — https://www.thelincolnforum.org/platt-family-essay-contest (OPEN TO FULL-TIME, UNDERGRADUATE STUDENTS IN AN AMERICAN COLLEGE OR UNIVERSITY. US CITIZENSHIP IS NOT REQUIRED.)		

Copyright © 2024
The Scholarship Workshop LLC • P. O. Box 176 • Centreville, Virginia 20122 • www.scholarshipworkshop.com

The Scholarship Monthly Planner

Notes

_____

_____

_____

_____

_____

_____

_____

_____

_____

_____

_____

_____

_____

_____

_____

_____

_____

_____

_____

_____

_____

_____

_____

_____

_____

_____

DON'T FORGET!

- Final deadline dates have red text.
- Submit your application at least 7 days before the deadline.
- Always look at least 1 month ahead to get prepared for upcoming deadlines.
- Hate writing? Start on your essay at least 1 month prior to the deadline.
- Need recommendations? Ask at least 4 weeks prior to the deadline. Follow-up! Also, many programs request recommendations electronically. Please let someone know you've provided their e-mail address for a recommendation, so they will be prepared for the e-mail request.
- As you download applications, organize them. You should have one folder for each month. Place applications in the appropriate folder for each month. For example, all applications that are due in December should be in a folder marked December.
- Check previous months for application download dates or activities you need to complete. These activities are shown in black text. Although you may be behind with some activities, the deadline date for a scholarship or award may not have passed.
- Research and include local, regional, and state based scholarships in your calendar.
- Research and include scholarships based on your interests, personal characteristics, and situation in your calendar.
- Request nominations with a letter and your résumé.

Copyright © 2024
The Scholarship Workshop LLC • P. O. Box 176 • Centreville, Virginia 20122 • www.scholarshipworkshop.com

The Scholarship Monthly Planner

Important Notes & Reminders

- The scholarship programs and awards shown in *The Scholarship Monthly Planner* may not represent all scholarships available to you. Those listed are generally available to a majority of students. Please conduct additional research to find scholarships in your community and state as well as those that apply to your situation and specific interests. To learn how to find additional scholarships, read *Winning Scholarships for College* or attend a workshop or online class conducted by Marianne Ragins. You can also visit www.scholarshipworkshop.com and refer to the scholarship search or scholarship help section as well as the books and resources section for more information about online searches.

- Deadline dates may have changed prior to or after the publication of *The Scholarship Monthly Planner*. Please use the information provided to check the most current deadline date. In some cases, the prior year's date may be included to give an approximate timeframe for the current year's deadline. *COVID-19 may also alter deadlines or the availability of a scholarship, award, or prize.*

- Scholarship and award programs may be discontinued at any time.

- Some programs and awards included in the planner require nominations before you can submit an application. Use the contact information to find out to how to be nominated for a scholarship or award. For more information on requesting nominations, read *Winning Scholarships for College,* which includes a nomination request letter and other information.

- Some dates in the planner list more than one scholarship or award program.

- All text in red indicates a scholarship or award deadline. Space does not allow indication of whether this is a postmark or receipt date. To ensure your application or entry is received within the appropriate timeframe, please visit the website shown for more information and submit your application at least 7 days prior to the date shown in the calendar.

The Scholarship Workshop LLC and Marianne Ragins have no control over the quality, safety or legality of the scholarships or awards shown nor the ability of the scholarship and award sponsors/providers to provide scholarships or awards. *The Scholarship Monthly Planner* may contain inaccuracies or typographical errors. The Scholarship Workshop LLC nor Marianne Ragins make no representations concerning the accuracy, reliability, completeness, or timeliness of any information included in *The Scholarship Monthly Planner*. The use of *The Scholarship Monthly Planner* is at your own risk. Changes are periodically made to *The Scholarship Monthly Planner* and may be made at any time.

THE SCHOLARSHIP WORKSHOP LLC DOES NOT WARRANT THAT ANY INFORMATION IN *THE SCHOLARSHIP MONTHLY PLANNER* WILL BE ERROR-FREE. THE CONTENT PROVIDED IN THE SCHOLARSHIP MONTHLY PLANNER IS PROVIDED ON AN "AS IS" BASIS WITHOUT ANY WARRANTIES OF ANY KIND. THE SCHOLARSHIP WORKSHOP LLC AND MARIANNE RAGINS, TO THE FULLEST EXTENT PERMITTED BY LAW, DISCLAIMS ALL WARRANTIES, WHETHER EXPRESS OR IMPLIED, INCLUDING THE WARRANTY OF MERCHANTABILITY, FITNESS FOR PARTICULAR PURPOSE AND NON-INFRINGEMENT. THE SCHOLARSHIP WORKSHOP LLC AND MARIANNE RAGINS MAKE NO WARRANTIES ABOUT THE ACCURACY, RELIABILITY, COMPLETENESS, OR TIMELINESS OF THE MATERIAL, REFERENCES, TEXT, GRAPHICS, AND WEBSITES.

Copyright © 2024

The Scholarship Workshop LLC • P. O. Box 176 • Centreville, Virginia 20122 • www.scholarshipworkshop.com

www.ingramcontent.com/pod-product-compliance
Lightning Source LLC
Chambersburg PA
CBHW042345030426
42335CB00030B/3459